CROW WITH N

IKKYŪ

15th CENTURY ZEN MASTER

VERSIONS BY STEPHEN BERG

Preface by Lucien Stryk

COPPER CANYON PRESS

The publication of this book was supported by a grant
from the National Endowment for the Arts.

ISBN-13: 978-1-55659-152-5
Library of Congress Catalog Card Number 88-63223

NOTE: The two anecdotes in the preface, about Ninagawa and
Shukō, and the two poems, "Void in Form" and "Form in
Void," translated by Lucien Stryk and Takashi Ikemoto, from
Zen: Poems, Prayers, Sermons, Anecdotes, Interviews (2nd
edition, 1981), are used with the permission of Swallow/Ohio
University Press. Ikkyū's death poem, given at the end of the
Preface, from *Zen Poems of China and Japan: The Crane's Bill*
(Evergreen Edition, 1987), translated by Lucien Stryk and
Takashi Ikemoto, is used with permission of Grove Press.

The typeface is Bodoni, set by The Typeworks.
Interior design: Tree Swenson

Copper Canyon Press is in residence with Centrum
at Fort Worden State Park.

COPPER CANYON PRESS
Box 271, Port Townsend, WA 98368
www.coppercanyonpress.org

FOR MASAO ABE & MY DEAR FRIEND JEFF

CROW WITH NO MOUTH

PREFACE

WHEN Ninagawa-Shinzaemon, linked verse poet and Zen devotee, heard that Ikkyū, abbot of the famous Daitokuji in Murasakino (violet field) of Kyoto, was a remarkable master, he desired to become his disciple. He called on Ikkyū, and the following dialogue took place at the temple entrance:

> IKKYŪ: Who are you?
> NINAGAWA: A devotee of Buddhism.
> IKKYŪ: You are from?
> NINAGAWA: Your region.
> IKKYŪ: Ah. And what's happening there these days?
> NINAGAWA: The crows caw, the sparrows twitter.
> IKKYŪ: And where do you think you are now?
> NINAGAWA: In a field dyed violet.
> IKKYŪ: Why?
> NINAGAWA: Miscanthus, morning glories, safflowers, chrysanthemums, asters.
> IKKYŪ: And after they're gone?
> NINAGAWA: It's Miyagino (field known for its autumn flowering).
> IKKYŪ: What happens in the field?
> NINAGAWA: The stream flows through, the wind sweeps over.

Amazed at Ninagawa's Zen-like speech, Ikkyū led him to his room and served him tea. Then he spoke the following impromptu verse:

> I want to serve
> You delicacies.
> Alas! the Zen sect
> Can offer nothing.

At which the visitor replied:

The mind which treats me
To nothing is the original void—
A delicacy of delicacies.

Deeply moved, the master said, "My son, you have learned much."

Speaking those words, perhaps Ikkyū recalled harsh treatment he received from his second master, Kasō Sōdon, in the very same circumstances. Kasō had ignored him completely while he waited five days outside his temple gate, then had disciples pour water over his head. It would have taken much more to discourage this would-be disciple. Finally Kasō agreed to take him on. It could not have been his kindly disposition that encouraged Ninagawa to approach Ikkyū, whose reputation was fierce. Rather all he heard of the great master, famed painter and poet, suggested such an approach might please Ikkyū, which proved to be the case for the fortunate Ninagawa.

Ikkyū Sōjun, according to traditional sources, was born in 1394, the natural child of the Emperor Go Komatsu and a favorite lady in waiting, of the Fujiwara clan, at the Kyoto court. The Empress, seething, it's told, had her banished to a low section of the city, where Ikkyū was born. At six the boy was sent for training to Kyoto's Ankokuji Temple. Precocious, by thirteen he was composing poems in Chinese, a poem, no less, daily. At fifteen he wrote lines that were recited everywhere. He was already extremely independent, something of a gadfly. There was much that bothered him about temple life, its pious snobbery over family connections, and he nettled fellow monks with his sharp comments.

By seventeen Ikkyū had a Zen master, Ken'ō, with whom he lived for four years, until Ken'ō's death. Ken'ō was known for modesty and compassionate concern for the welfare of his disciples, and his loss affected Ikkyū profoundly. In comparison with Ken'ō, other Zen masters seemed ridiculously ostentatious and, in matters of temple ritual, nitpicking. Seeking another master, Ikkyū chose a severe disciplinarian of the Rinzai sect named Kasō Sōdon. He was of the Daitokuji Temple line, whose distinguished lineage led to Hakuin (1686–1769), among its greatest heirs. While Kasō was aware of the importance of such lineage, and performed his abbot's duties faithfully, he preferred living in a small temple in Kataka, a short distance from Kyoto on the shore of Lake Biwa.

When twenty-five, Ikkyū, hearing a song from the *Heike Monogatari*, suddenly penetrated a kōan (Zen problem for meditation) given him by Kasō, and he always was to speak of the moment as his first *kenshō* (awakening). But a more profound experience came two years later. While meditating in a boat on Lake Biwa, hearing a crow call, he was immediately, fully enlightened.

He hurried to Kasō for approval of his *satori*, but the master said, "This is the enlightenment of a mere *arhat*, you're no master yet." Ikkyū replied, "Then I'm happy to be an *arhat*, I detest masters." At which Kasō declared, "Ha, now you really *are* a master."

After his awakening Ikkyū stayed with the master, taking care of him in growing illness, a paralysis of the lower limbs that necessitated his being carried everywhere. Ikkyū's unflagging loyalty impressed all, became legendary:

> my dying teacher could not wipe himself unlike you disciples
> who use bamboo I cleaned his lovely ass with my bare hands

Kasō died when Ikkyū was thirty-five, and the bereaved monk, who at the darkest moment of mourning had been close to suicide, began an endless round of travel, lasting the remainder of his life. He could not settle anywhere, and his behavior, even in those bawdy times, was thought scandalous. He never pretended to be saintly, took his passions as a natural part of life, frankly loved *sake* and women. After a disappointing day he would rush from the temple to a bar, wind up at a brothel. After which there was often a crisis of self-doubt, if not guilt. At such moments he went to his hermitage in the mountains at Joo:

> ten years of whorehouse joy I'm alone now in the mountains
> the pines are like a jail the wind scratches my skin

Ikkyū also had a hermitage in Kyoto which he called Katsuroan (Blind Donkey Hermitage), and often stayed at Daitokuji. But increasingly, to the point of anguish, he became disgusted with worldly carryings on at the main temple, shuddered at the business side of its affairs, and felt intense enmity toward Kasō's successor, Yōsō. Twenty years his senior, Yōsō represented all Ikkyū despised in Rinzai practices of the day, among them frantic hustling for donations:

> Yōsō hangs up ladles baskets useless donations in the temple
> my style's a straw raincoat strolls by rivers and lakes

> *   *   *

> ten fussy days running this temple all red tape
> look me up if you want to in the bar whorehouse fish
> market

In 1471, when seventy-seven, Ikkyū revealed his passion for a blind girl, an attendant at the Shūon'an Temple at Takigi. He wrote poems about their affair, some farcical, some very moving. He was self-conscious at the oddness of an old Zen monk falling for a young woman, but they spent years together, Ikkyū's feeling for her growing in intensity;

> I love taking my new girl blind Mori on a spring picnic
> I love seeing her exquisite free face its moist sexual heat
> shine

> *   *   *

> your name Mori means *forest* like the infinite fresh
> green distances of your blindness

When Ikkyū reached the age of eighty-two, far steadier, much becalmed, he was made abbot of Daitokuji, and often expressed childlike wonderment at his elevation, given his unorthodox behavior throughout his long life, to a position so lofty. Though he appeared to revel in his unexpected role, he was often away from Daitokuji, mostly at his beloved Shūon'an Temple where he died in 1482, at eighty-eight.

While it may be that Ikkyū is best known in the Zen world as a sort of rake, always spitting in the face of orthodoxy, madly carrying on as freest of the free, most of his poems are concerned with Zen, revered to this day by Zennists. Among the best-known of such poems are two based on the concepts "Void in Form" and "Form in Void" as given in the *Hridaya* (Heart Sutra), one of the major sutras of Buddhism and of great importance to the Zen sect:

VOID IN FORM
When, just as they are,
White dewdrops gather
On scarlet maple leaves,
Regard the scarlet beads!

* * *

FORM IN VOID
The tree is stripped,
All color, fragrance gone,
Yet already on the bough,
Uncaring spring!

As indication of the importance to the Zen community of such pieces, I was constantly reminded by my collaborator, the late Takashi Ikemoto, while translating these two poems, of their spiritual and metaphysical significance. They were to be just so, and we turned the phrasing over and over. We were fully conscious of the range of Ikkyū's life and art, making no excuses for his unconventional behavior but insisting on approaching him as illustrious master, one whose insight guided so many disciples.

Among those who came to him for guidance was Murata Shukō, the most eminent tea ceremony master of the day. Visiting Ikkyū, he was asked what he thought of Master Joshu's well-known reference to tea drinking (in spite of their different responses, Joshu invariably said to three monks training under him, "Have a cup of tea"). Shukō remained silent, and at last Ikkyū served him a cup of tea.

As Shukō lifted the cup to his lips, Ikkyū let out with a Zen shout and smashed the cup with his iron *nyoi* (Buddhist implement).

Shukō made a deep bow.

"What are you like," Ikkyū said, "when you've no intention of taking tea?"

Without answering, Shukō got up and moved toward the door.

"Stop," Ikkyū called. "What are you like when you've taken tea?"

"The willow is green," Shukō said, "the rose is red."

Ikkyū, approving Shukō's grasp of Zen, smiled broadly.

Throughout his life Ikkyū took his Zen responsibilities, the temple rituals and later, disciples, conscientiously, in spite of his marked independence, but he would suddenly get fed up with routine, heading for the hills:

> when I was 47 everyone came to see me
> so I walked out forever

Once, in utter disgust with the Zen community's catering to the privileged, its blindness to raw truth, he destroyed his *inka*, his master's formal written testimony to his enlightenment, his major qualification to serve as master:

one of you saved my satori paper I know it piece by piece
>you
pasted it back together now watch me burn it once and for
>all

With that by now typical gesture, I imagine, Ikkyū probably rushed from the temple to the nearest bar, followed by a night in the brothel.

What are we, centuries, worlds away from Ikkyū, to make of his extraordinary life? The Japanese, with few exceptions, have been equally puzzled. He has perhaps as many apologists as followers—it would be wrong to imagine that they are more forgiving than we of eccentricity and "turpitude." And though they have made allowances for Zen behavior, just as the Chinese in the T'ang Dynasty did for Taoist ways, there are clear limits to their tolerance, as much today as in the past. Yet it is his total freedom that makes him such an appealing figure. What is wrong about delighting in the body, its natural needs, on what authority is sex condemnable? If one avoids giving pain, if one abides by what is virtually Buddhism's golden rule, to live inoffensively, why not live passionately?

There is a touching side to Crazy Cloud, as he was known and often referred to himself. It has to do with what is known in modern clinical parlance as "erotic renewal," and it was something he was not only aware of but most grateful for:

>I was like an old leafless tree until we met green buds burst
>>and blossom
>now that I have you I'll never forget what I owe you

>>>*   *   *

>white-haired priest in his eighties
>Ikkyū still sings aloud each night to himself to the sky to the
>>clouds
>because she gave herself freely
>her hands her mouth her breasts her long moist thighs

Not only Ikkyū, in fulfillment, had much to thank his young blind lover for, but Zennists everywhere owe her a debt, for in the fullest sense she perked up his life, inspired his days, keeping ever clear his Zen mind. A mind so sharp that even at the very end, when as all masters of his day he brushed his death poem, he couldn't resist just one more barb:

> South of Mount Sumeru
> Who understands my Zen?
> Call Master Kido over—
> He's not worth a cent.

Crow with No Mouth: Ikkyū is a most welcome collection of many of Ikkyū's strongest and most revealing poems, rendered in very free and highly spirited versions by Stephen Berg, Ikkyū's fellow poet. It is a collection to rejoice over and, I feel confident, would have mightily pleased Crazy Cloud himself.

– LUCIEN STRYK

FOREWORD

HARSH, delicate, brilliant, reckless, precise, intimate, ignorant, arrogant, aloof—Ikkyū comes across as a man of simultaneously miserable self-doubt and infinite self-confidence. He is always bent on crushing any ideal of self or conduct, any theory or belief. His core, his "real self" as it has been called, the "true man of no rank" is an anonymous force whose successive conditions are the same moment-by-moment states of fluid nameless identity we can sense in ourselves. Or say that Ikkyū's nature and Nature are synonymous. Listening to fishermen, playing with a lover, expounding a fleeting splinter of thought, the man is all there. He is never a "half-filled mask," Rilke's term for us when we evade ourselves as we are. Jung's "The most terrifying thing is to accept oneself completely" is enacted by Ikkyū in the poems that track his life and the life of his mind. Kawabata calls him "the most severe and profound" teacher, perhaps because he leaves no part of himself unrevealed; because of his attempt at moral, spiritual, and personal inclusiveness. Wherever he is, whoever he is, he is relentlessly frank, naked, sincere, skilled in the uses of suffering. The long explosion of his character continues with equal intensity to the end of his life. Strangers at first, possibly we discovered a lost acquaintance – it happened in a flash, couplet after couplet. They say everyone meets himself in Ikkyū, immediately, in his deep fund of passion.

Without Ikkyū's poetry in translations by James H. Sanford, Sonja Arntzen, and Jon Carter Covell with Sobin Yamada my versions would not have been possible. Their books explore the man's life through firm literal English poems and commentaries that became my literary source.

Ikkyū wrote in a four-line form. My couplets (with a few exceptions) came as a necessary skeleton for the work of inspiring a voice whose first notes caught me when I read the scholars' books. A true essay about what happened between their texts and mine would have to explain at length a process not usually associated with other such ambitious transfigurations. For now, let me thank W.S. Merwin and Lucien Stryk for their suggestions.

– STEPHEN BERG

CROW WITH NO MOUTH

Hearing a crow with no mouth
Cry in the deep
Darkness of the night,
I feel a longing for
My father before he was born.

from A ZEN HARVEST

translated by Sōiku Shigematsu

even before trees rocks I was nothing
when I'm dead nowhere I'll be nothing

all the bad things I do will go up in smoke
and so will I

if there's nowhere to rest at the end
how can I get lost on the way?

this ink painting of wind blowing through pines
who hears it?

born born everything is always born
thinking about it try not to

poetry's hellish bullshit one good way to suffer men love it
men stupid as horses cows

sexual love's attachment pain is deeper than I can know
wind soothes my thoughts this lust my ceaseless koan
impossibly happy

outrageous eyes ears nose in the cold one silent tinkling bell
clear beautiful nudged by the wind hangs over the polished
    railing

sin like a madman until you can't do anything else
no room for any more

night after night after night stay up all night
nothing but your own night

believe in the man facing you now
just narrow your eyes feel the deep love

raining or not
walk lifting your heavy wet sleeves

I can't smell a thing can't see their pink
but they'll find branches next spring

fuck flattery success money
all I do is lie back suck my thumb

so many words about it
the only language is you don't open your lips

no walls no roof no anything my house
doesn't get wet doesn't get blown down

you can hear it when it doesn't even move
you can hear it when the wind forces itself past rocks

clouds very high look
not one word helped them get up there

a well nobody dug filled with no water
ripples and a shapeless weightless man drinks

this world this thing you and I call knowing
those ten words these fifty-four-year-old fingers are everything

here I am simply trying to get into your head
you think you were born you die what a pity

like a knifeblade the moon will be full then less
than nothing but it's dawn and the moon's a knifeblade

oh green green willow wonderfully red flower
but I know the colors are not there

one long pure beautiful road of pain
and the beauty of death and no pain

you won't even be here to read them
what stupidity to put these words in your mouth

nobody told the flowers to come up nobody
will ask them to leave when spring's gone

I didn't see one thing on my trip
but I breathed and whatever I breathed was time

my gray cat jumped up just as I lifted this spoon
we're born we die

that stone Buddha deserves all the birdshit it gets
I wave my skinny arms like a tall flower in the wind

it isn't that we're alone or not alone
whose voice do you want mine? yours?

I won't die I won't go away I'll always be here
no good asking me I won't speak

you poor sad thing thinking death is real
all by itself

only a kind deadly sincere man
can show you the way here in the other world

I'm in it everywhere
what a miracle trees lakes clouds even dust

I'd love to give you something
but what would help?

melons eggplants rice rivers the sky
I offer them to you on this holiday

Ikkyū this body isn't yours I say to myself
wherever I am I'm there

my mind can't answer when you call
if it did I'd be stealing your life from you

oh yes things exist like the echo when you yell at the foot of a
huge mountain

hear the cruel no-answer until blood drips down
beat your head against the wall of it

pleasure pain are equal in a clear heart
no mountain hides the moon

this boat is and is not
when it sinks both disappear

I'm pure shame
what I do and what I say never the same

you can't be anyone but you
therefore you are that Other one you love

———

no tiny wooden hut with a grass roof in the hills
but this city these people where I live still are impossible

mirror facing a mirror
nowhere else

on the deep green lily pad dew
has no color of its own

the mind is exactly this tree that grass
without thought or feeling both disappear

wife daughters friends this is for you satori
is mistake after mistake

before birth after birth
that's where you are now

I try to be a good man but all that comes
of trying is I feel more guilty

not two not one either
and the unpainted breeze in the ink painting feels cool

—

I like my anger my grouchy furious love
amazing how we say such nice things about the dead

this brick house I live in is really the sky
and just as priceless

you me when I think really think about it
are the same

go down on your silly knees pray
for what? tomorrow *is* yesterday

don't worry please please how many times do I have to say it
there's no way not to be who you are and where

all koans just lead you on
but not the delicious pussy of the young girls I go down on

thirsty you dream of water cold you want fire
not me I want the firm warm breasts and wetness of a woman

I found my sparrow Sonrin dead one morning
and dug his grave as gently as I would my own daughter's

you can't make cherry blossoms by tearing off petals
to plant only spring does that

clouds endless clouds climbing beyond
ask nothing from words on a page

keep writing those deep questions sleep on
when you wake even you'll be gone

sometimes all I am is a dark emptiness
I can't hide in the sleeves of my own robes

October wind crosses the world
in this field moist grass bends to itself and to the sea

I'm alive! right? don't we say that?
we don't see the bones we walk on

gravestones melt to stumps of stone knobs
use them to grind tea leaves

lone moon no clouds
we stumble through the night

long life
the wild pines want it too

I hate it I know it's nothing but I
suck out the world's sweet juicy plum

why is it all so beautiful this fake dream
this craziness why?

nobody before me nobody after
writing it

nobody knows shit nobody lives anywhere
hello dust!

so many paths go up from the foothills
but one moon grazes the peak

it's logical: if you're not going anywhere
any road is the right one

rain hail snow ice
I love watching the river

pine needles inches deep hug the ground
no one lives here

my friend's funeral this morning
burns inside me like my own death

and it breaks my heart how so easily
smoke rises tonight like the thought of him

they could have put a small doll in the urn
but it was my father's ashes

know nothing I know nothing nobody does can you face me
  and know nothing know

icy window windy snow moon tangled among black flowers
the mind is water wrapping itself where it is around what what
    what
never the same

oh the evening wind hurries smoke our smoke
into the sky

stare at it until your eyes drop out
this desk this wall this unreal page

———

Yoso hangs up ladles baskets useless donations in the temple
my style's a straw raincoat strolls by rivers and lakes

ten fussy days running this temple all red tape
look me up if you want to in the bar whorehouse fish market

nature's a killer I won't sing to it
I hold my breath and listen to the dead singing under the
    grass

I live in a shack on the edge of whorehouse row
me autumn a single candle

one half-thawed lovesong chilly as dusk remains
my life stalking hills now these shameful purple robes

talk about family laws ideals my silence drives me mad
without passion and ignorance none of it works

up all night in this fisherman's hut drinking talking
his wife hates me bangs her spoon on the kettle

chopping up herbs blood flows from my hand into the block
no food my teacher mocks me with a smile

stirring cold ashes with his eyes shut tight
another student weeps into the sparks

another house has its own path through the dark
what about when moss grows on the heart's road

my dying teacher could not wipe himself unlike you disciples
who use bamboo I cleaned his lovely ass with my bare hands

ten dumb years I wanted things to be different furious proud I
    still feel it
one summer midnight in my little boat on Lake Biwa
    caaaawwweeeee
father when I was a boy you left us now I forgive you

the edges of the sword are life and death
no one knows which is which

even in its scabbard my sword
sees you

I don't own a sewing needle but I keep calligraphy
in a special box given by my dying friend

in a dazzling scabbard
this wooden sword
which can't kill or help you to live

suddenly nothing but grief
so I put on my father's old ripped raincoat

brown ruffle of flame rushes across my white paper diploma
why tie up the donkey

when I was forty-seven everybody came to see me
so I walked out forever

her mouth played with my cock
the way a cloud plays with the sky

I'm up here in the hills starving myself
but I'll come down for you

one of you saved my satori paper I know it piece by piece you
pasted it back together now watch me burn it once and for all

this soul torch I hold up lights the sky
think of those nights freezing staring into the river

my monk friend has a weird endearing habit
he weaves sandals and leaves them secretly by the roadside

look up Heaven look around you Earth red flesh white bones
     crushed
between both the real you survives

I love bamboo how it looks
and because men carve it into flutes

Ikkyū near death returns your cloak to you
slash it in half it's still yours

where you are whatever you do
hearing a stalk struck remember bamboo remembers nothing

it takes horseshit to grow bamboo
and it too longs forever weeps begs to the wind

night plum blossoms spreading under a branch
between her thighs narcissus revolves smell it?

a crazy lecher shuttling between whorehouse and bar
this past master paints south north east west with his cock

they do it in the street in broad daylight like cows and horses
it's late the moon goes under west of Ch'ang-an

all the old masters want is money and fame
strike like a feather but when

they screw inside the temple call in students for "mysterious
    satori"
only I teach like the seasons

sick Zen from the famous three you know who I mean
I can change your life with a mere look

they used sticks and yells and other tricks those fakes
Ikkyū reaches high low like sunlight

flowers are silent silence is silent the mind
is a silent flower the silent flower of the world opens

six years of hunger sitting like a secret in darkness
his bones pierced with the less-and-less the near-nothing

a flower held up twirled between human fingers
a smile barely visible

frogs at the bottom of a well like you idiot
thrashing in mud laughable so very very right

something in us always wants to cry out
someone we love knows hears

this useless dying koan body singing its lust
weeds not yet cleared everywhere

raging in the now hungry for it
crows rattle the air no dust

no nothing only those wintry crows
bright black in the sun

listen whose face is it a piece
of sunlit jade warbling laughing

one pause between each crow's
reckless shriek Ikkyū Ikkyū Ikkyū

rice boils in my broken-footed iron pot
it's everything but you can't taste it

peace isn't luck for six years stand facing a silent wall
until the you of your face melts like a candle

don't wait for the man standing in the snow
to cut off his arm help him now

some monks live in caves build huts on snowy mountains
right now clouds flee across the moon my heart

we're lost born in delusions deeper than any mind
if you could escape awakening you'd ripen like a pear all by
    itself

three-foot axe leans on the headsman's block
cuts through deep feelings April

amazingly sad how its blade mirrors the years
how sadness extends far as the hills and rivers

so burning's knowing and I'm not even drunk on three wines
plunge into the fire reality pure endless pain

one white blossom snow
razor-edged mountains slice my belly

I have to admit my passion never leaves
fire is the master young grasses appear each spring

don't hesitate get laid that's wisdom
sitting around chanting what crap

we're lost where the mind can't find us
utterly lost

Lin-chi screamed KATSU! at precisely the right time gave life
    death KATSU!
eyes everywhere blazing blazing eyes sun moon KATSU!
    KATSU!

beloved Wei-shan wanted to come back as a cow grazing in a
    wide valley
can't you see him munching flowers idling under stars on a
    windy night

life's like climbing knife-trees hills with swords sticking up
day and night something stabs you

we live in a cage of light an amazing cage
animals animals without end

sick all I can think of is love and fucking the love song
hums in my groin listen my hair's white wild grasses uncut on
    my meadow

chrysanthemums hammered out of raw iron
that cloud gone now like my father

---

sick of it whatever it's called sick of the names
I dedicate every pore to what's here

I'd sniff you like a dog and taste you
then kiss your other mouth endlessly if I could white hair
or not

Lin-chi's followers don't know Zen I the Blind Donkey do
my tongue and gentle fingers thick hard cock
one autumn night's a thousand centuries

nobody cares about my hungers thirsts
smash the plum blossom's one night's ice

no money in a dream plums simple and close
five thousand coins in a row in a dream of power

inside the koan clear mind
gashes the great darkness

in deep winter I write poems get drunk the cup's heavier
    heavier moon
whispering all night even at sixty I'm hard in her again and
    again

Ikkyū the whole day singing boozing so great so
fully here he built a bridge no one uses 10,000 miles long

I went half crazy studying sitting for days now the one thing
is fishermen's songs sunset rain clouds the river night after
      night

ten years of whorehouse joy I'm alone now in the mountains
the pines are like a jail the wind scratches my skin

I'm like wind pouring down hills into the city
whatever I do is beyond whatever's been done

the crow's *caw* was ok but one night with a lovely whore
opened a wisdom deeper than what that bird said

cheap tea thin gruel pale leaves as winter begins
this threadbare robe feels fine in the first dawn frost

Zen's finished stick your brain in a peach branch guzzle *sake*
sing until you have no throat then words come by themselves

brush ink plunge forward blind man who knows each step in
    the dark
the bristles dry dip again brush blind until you're gone

break open the cherry tree where's the flower?
but spring

in war there's no time to teach or learn Zen carry a strong
    stick
bash your attackers

who brought these fish sizzling in the pan I'll never stop
    thinking
about women white hair lust sings through my body weeds
    everywhere

skinny legs wandering no friends the lamppost moves not me
    following my song
money is power spring the cuckoo weeps blood inside me

watching my four-year-old daughter dance
I can't break free of her

it's a hungry morning when I don't see her
more and more I love her and drink wine more

I've burnt all the holy pages I used to carry
but poems flare in my heart

the wise know nothing at all
well maybe one song

empty belly no wine it's freezing
melody the angel's shining cloak stains the air

———

alone with the icy moon no passion
these trees this mountain nothing else

nobody understands my not no Zen Zen
not even that crow's shattering bleak scream got it

break through one impasse there's another let the sweet
lychee slip over your tongue and down

a beautiful woman's hot vagina's full of love
I've given up trying to put out the fire of my body

if you don't break rules you're an ass not human
women start us passion comes and goes until death

I love taking my new girl blind Mori on a spring picnic
I love seeing her exquisite free face its moist sexual heat shine

your name Mori means *forest* like the infinite fresh
green distances of your blindness

how is my hand like Mori's?
it's her freedom I love when I'm sick she makes me hard
fingers lips rove everywhere bring my followers joy

I'm whole as long as I hear you singing
then emptiness when you stop

a woman is enlightenment when you're with her and the red
thread
of both your passions flares inside you and you see

I remember one quiet afternoon she fished out my cock
bent over played with it in her mouth for at least an hour

for us no difference between reading eating singing
making love not one thing or the other

once while she was cooking I kneeled put my head between
　　her warm dark legs
up her skirt kissed and licked and sucked her until she came

she'd play with it almost anywhere day and night
touch it with the deepest part of herself

and the nights inside you rocking
smelling the odor of your thighs is everything

I think of your death think of us touching
my head quiet in your lap

I was like an old leafless tree until we met green buds burst
    and blossom
now that I have you I'll never forget what I owe you

plum blossom close to the ground her dark place opens
wet with the dew of her passion wet with the lust of my tongue

white-haired priest in his eighties
Ikkyū still sings aloud each night to himself to the sky the
    clouds
because she gave herself freely
her hands her mouth her breasts her long moist thighs

some die meditating some on their feet but he did both
not black not white that old mad man P'u-K'o
like a distant bird barely audible

Hsu-T'ang tore off his robes like a broken sandal
Zen has no center clouds rake the moon some voice claws at
    my heart

this morning's koan's a poem tonight people flock to this
    mountain
I live the problem ignore poor birds pleading for food

only one koan matters
you

poetry's ridiculous write it feel proud
strut look in the mirror believe you know

sutras poems I stash them under my robe burn them all
but not words written on my heart

flute notes bring gods demons only that music
again the world's biggest ass-man hasn't one friend
his loneliness that music

I walked through the door of death came back went back am
          here
brisk wind warm rain dawn the bleached moon

you stand inside me naked infinite love
the dawn bell rips my dreaming heart

books koans sitting miss the heart but not fishermen's songs
rain pelts the river I sing beyond all of it

who teaches truth? good/bad the wrong way
Crazy Cloud knows the taste of his own shit
long love letters brief passionate poems

this hungry monk chanting by lamplight is Buddha
and he still thinks of you

a butterfly hovers in front of her face
how long will she sleep

one wisp rootless shifting a dot in the blue sky
know it

anybody can enter Buddha's world
so few can step into the Devil's

I ask you answer I don't you don't
O Lord Bodidharma what's in your unknown heart

and what *is* the heart
pine breeze voice in a forgotten painting

this cow has come to teach you: what you do is where you are
where you are is what you do: nobody knows which monk I
    was

no more Zen write one great line
like a needle piercing a sore spot on your arm

in the freezing hall one night in a flimsy robe I hallucinated
      gold-threaded cloth
it hung in the air uselessly

those old koans meaningless just ways of faking virtue
this gorgeous young whore wears silk robes that hang open
    about an inch

Crazy Cloud likes his own mind its wish for flutesongs rainy
     nights
drinking muttering beside his women

the girl listening to the poet bursting with poems thinks
     nothing
but he thinks he wants her leaning on the gate while she just
     listens

I'm eighty still alive looking up every night
snapping my fingsers at time at the promise of love

   at the bath she bathed scrubbing her face and body
   at the bath I splashed water on myself enjoying her body

hundreds of peaks but only one lone bell out of nowhere
maple groves tipped by stars fixed above the inlet

nobody knows I'm a storm I'm
dawn on the mountain twilight on the town

poems should come from bare ground
night falling on night falling on a black landscape

Rinzai did it without a care
no clouds wind sky a heart that simply sings

eat the wind eat the water nobody can say how
I know a man who stood twenty years on Gojo bridge

stand tiptoe on the tip of a needle
like a grain of sand flashing in sunlight

my name Ikkyū's disgusting not dust yet
it should be swept away and will be

nobody understands why we do what we do
this cup of *sake* does

age eighty weak
I shit and offer it to Buddha

even if Buddha himself kneeled at my deathbed
he wouldn't be worth shit

self other right wrong wasting your life arguing
you're happy really you *are* happy

forget what the masters wrote truth's a razor
each instant sitting here you and I being here

no masters only you the master is you
wonderful no?

men are like cows horses fuck poetry
look at your hand read it

even Rinzai's disciples don't know
so many ordinary people know but don't know they know
walking to work talking to themselves

I still worry about how I look my dry white hair oh
age wanting to fuck but I'll sing no matter how things are

rain drips from the roof lip
loneliness sounds like that

passion's red thread is infinite
like the earth always under me

this donkey stumbles blind over stones into walls ditches
no words for grief or joy no words for his ruined heart

cut off everything from everything stand here the soles of your
    feet the ground
your brain in the black nothing between

I woke from a dream of death to day's amazing
death grass death rice death chairs death death asleep or
    awake

no words sitting alone night in my hut eyes closed hands open
wisps of an unknown face

my death? who was it anyway always where he was never
no not once ever seeing himself an eyeball speaks

ABOUT THE TRANSLATOR

Stephen Berg is the author of several volumes of poetry including *The Daughters, Grief, With Akhmatova at the Black Gates,* and most recently, *In It,* as well as versions from Nahuatl, *Nothing in the Word,* and versions of Eskimo songs, *Sea Ice.* His translations include poems of the modern Hungarian Miklos Radnoti, *Clouded Sky* (with Stephen Polgar and S.J. Marks) and Sophocles's *Oedipus the King* (with Diskin Clay). He was the editor (with Robert Mezey) of the highly acclaimed *Naked Poetry* anthologies.

Berg is founder (in 1971) and co-editor of *The American Poetry Review.* He has been awarded the Frank O'Hara Memorial Prize, a Guggenheim Fellowship in Poetry, a National Endowment for the Arts Fellowship, a National Translation Center Grant from the Ford Foundation, a Rockefeller Fellowship, and a Columbia University Translation Prize. He has taught at Princeton and Haverford, and is currently Professor of English at the University of the Arts in Philadelphia.